TO THE EXTREME

Mountain Biking

by Sarah L. Schuette

Reading Consultant:
Barbara J. Fox
Reading Specialist
North Carolina State University

Capstone press

Mankato, Minnesota

Blazers is published by Capstone Press,
151 Good Counsel Drive, P.O. Box 669, Mankato, Minnesota 56002.
www.capstonepress.com

Library of Congress Cataloging-in-Publication Data
Schuette, Sarah L., 1976–
    Mountain biking / by Sarah L. Schuette
    p. cm.—(Blazers—to the extreme)
    Includes bibliographical references and index.
    ISBN 0-7368-3787-6 (hardcover)
    1. All terrain cycling—Juvenile literature. I. Title. II. Series.
GV1056.S38 2005
796.6'3—dc22   2004016858

Summary: Describes the sport of mountain biking, including
    equipment and safety information.

Credits
Jason Knudson, set designer; Enoch Peterson and Steve Christensen,
    book designers; Kelly Garvin, photo researcher; Scott Thoms,
    photo editor

Photo Credits
Chuck Haney, 24–25, 26–27
Corbis/Duomo/Paul J. Sutton, 21; RNT Productions, 28–29
Getty Images Inc./Adam Petty, 16–17; Doug Pensinger, 13; Nathan
    Bilow, 18; Nick Laham, 19
Houserstock/Christie Parker, 4–5, 6–7, 8–9; Ellen Barone, 14–15
Raw Talent Photo/J. Blackman, 10–11
SportsChrome Inc./Sport the Library/Dan Campbell, cover, 20,
    22–23; Tom Moran, 12

1 2 3 4 5 6 10 09 08 07 06 05

Table of Contents

Adventure Riding

A mountain biker races along a trail. He pedals hard to catch the leader. He struggles up a rocky hill.

He sees the leader up ahead.
Suddenly, another racer challenges
for the lead. He pedals harder and
shifts gears.

He passes the other riders around the final curve. Pedaling harder, he finishes the race and takes first place.

BLAZER FACT

People called the first mountain bikes clunkers.

Equipment

Mountain bikes travel on rough ground. Their frames must be strong but not heavy. Tires with wide treads help keep riders on course.

Riders shift gears on the
handlebars to help them climb
steep hills. They stand and pedal
until they reach the top.

Mountain Bike Diagram

Handlebars

Tire

Helmet

Pedal

Racing

Mountain bikers race downhill or cross-country. Cross-country racers ride on tracks, through forests, and over rocky areas.

Riders sometimes carry their
bikes up hills. At the top, they
jump on again and race down
the other side.

Downhill racers speed over jumps and around corners. Crashes happen when obstacles can't be avoided quickly enough.

Safety

Long sleeves and long pants help keep downhill racers safe. Other mountain bikers wear light clothing to stay cool in hot weather.

Helmets protect bikers from hurting their heads during crashes. Sport glasses keep dirt and the sun out of riders' eyes.

BLAZER FACT

Downhill racers can reach speeds of 60 miles (97 kilometers) per hour.

Rough ground is hard on a mountain bike. Tires often blow out. Bikers carry tools to fix problems along a course.

BLAZER FACT

Most bikers carry first aid kits to treat cuts and scrapes.

Let's ride

Glossary

course (KORSS)—a route; some mountain bikers travel on courses with trails through rough areas.

frame (FRAYM)—the main body of a mountain bike

gear (GIHR)—a set of wheels with metal teeth that fit together to help a bike move

obstacle (OB-stuh-kuhl)—an object that stands in a mountain biker's way

tread (TRED)—the ridges on a tire

Read More

Deady, Kathleen W. *Extreme Mountain Biking Moves.* Behind the Moves. Mankato, Minn.: Capstone Press, 2003.

Kelley, K. C. *Mountain Biking.* Extreme Sports. Milwaukee: Gareth Stevens, 2004.

Rosenberg, Aaron. *Mountain Biking: Techniques and Tricks.* Rad Sports. New York: Rosen, 2003.

Internet Sites

FactHound offers a safe, fun way to find Internet sites related to this book. All of the sites on FactHound have been researched by our staff.

Here's how:

1. Visit *www.facthound.com*
2. Type in this special code **0736837876** for age-appropriate sites. Or enter a search word related to this book for a more general search.
3. Click on the **Fetch It** button.

FactHound will fetch the best sites for you!

Index